STATI
for a
NEW MILLENNIUM

Alexius Healy OFM Cap

ST PAULS

ACKNOWLEDGEMENTS

Scripture quotations: Christian Community Bible,
Catholic Pastoral Edition – © Sociedad Biblica Catolica
Internacional, Madrid (1988). Publishers ST PAULS

Photography: Sr Rosaleen McCabe OSC

Manuscript preparation: Aideen Foley

Iconography: Sr John Francis PC

Cover illustration "Highlighting the suffering face of Jesus" is
from the Capuchin Chapel, Carlow, Ireland.

ST PAULS Publishing
187 Battersea Bridge Road, London SW11 3AS, UK

ISBN 085439 571 7
First published 2000, Reprinted 2000, 2001

Set by TuKan DTP, Fareham, UK
Produced in the EC
Printed by AGAM, Cuneo, Italy

ST PAULS is an activity of the priests and brothers
of the Society of St Paul who proclaim the Gospel
through the media of social communication

Introduction

The Way of the Cross is Franciscan in origin. When his early followers asked St Francis of Assisi to teach them about prayer, he told them that all the lessons they would ever need on prayer could be read on the Cross of the Lord. From this developed the devotion of meditation and prayer around fourteen of the incidents in the passion and death of Jesus.

It is true that Christ's passion can help us to cope with our own hardships and difficulties. Under the weight of so much modern stress, the prayerful remembrance of Calvary may well be the only motive left for remaining steadfast and faithful to God.

For me, the Stations of the Cross are a meditation on life. As we begin this New Millennium we can contemplate the human tragedy of modern Golgothas. Today Jesus continues his painful journey among our brothers and sisters who are being abandoned, aborted, hounded and persecuted. Given the trauma of ethnic cleansing, the enforced displacement of millions, wherever the culture of death prevails, Christ, the Messiah, is repeatedly humiliated and mocked in the victims of hatred and evil in every time and place.

In offering these meditations I recall Pope John Paul's words as he led the Stations of the Cross at Rome's Coliseum on Good Friday 1999. He commended this New Millennium into the hands of God, recalling the last words of Christ on the cross, *'Into your hands, O Lord, I commend my spirit. In the light of the mounting uneasiness and pressures of modern life, we can only commend ourselves into the safe and caring hands of Almighty God. All history is his. Empires and kingdoms come and go, but the Lord lasts forever'* (John Paul II).

The message of this New Millennium is that human sin can be forgiven through the blood of the innocent Lord. Strong hope must always defeat the temptation to despair. The cross of Christ is a torch of hope that keeps alive the expectation of a new day of resurrection. Christ is risen! May this booklet enable you to pray the Way of the Cross with sincerity and devotion.

Alexius Healy OFM Cap
Capuchin Franciscan
Lent 2000

Opening Prayer

LORD,

We are about to walk in prayer the Way of the Cross with you. May we travel with you firm in the faith, loyal to the truth, obedient to the will of the Father, along the one true path that leads to life. As we celebrate this New Millennium open our hearts to the richness of our faith. Open our minds to its meaning. We adore you and bless you as Our Lord and Saviour, the Way, the Truth and the Life. Through your passion and death may we be brought to the glory of the resurrection.

FIRST STATION
Jesus is condemned to death

I

The chief priests and the guards cried out, 'Crucify him! Crucify him!' Pilate replied, 'Take him yourselves and have him crucified, for I find no case against him.'

John 19:6

We adore you, Lord Jesus Christ
and we bless you,
because by your holy cross
you have redeemed the world.

This is a scene found today in many countries torn apart by war and bloodshed. In Jerusalem there are riots, marches and protests. Terrorists pave the streets. Shouts of 'crucify him, crucify him' ring again loud and clear. Suddenly there is a hushed silence. Christ appears at the door of Pilate's court-room – a man alone and condemned. Pressure groups have won the day. Jesus must die, a human life must be destroyed.

LORD,

Grant us the grace not to condemn life but to accept and respect it. Human life is sacred from womb to tomb; no motive can ever make its destruction right. May we celebrate the dignity of every person to whom God has given the gift of life, not only the strong and the healthy but especially those who are vulnerable: the little child in the womb, the elderly in our nursing homes, the person suffering from illness or disability. May the gift of your Spirit lead us to recognise, across all cultures and frontiers, the faces of our brothers and sisters, children of God, our Father in heaven.

> *Dying you destroyed our death.*
> *Rising you restored our life.*
> *Lord Jesus, come in glory.*

SECOND STATION
Jesus accepts his cross

Then Pilate handed Jesus over to them to be crucified. They took charge of him. Bearing his own
cross, Jesus went out of the city to what is called
the Place of the Skull, in Hebrew: *Golgotha*.

John 19:16-17

We adore you, Lord Jesus Christ
and we bless you,
because by your holy cross
you have redeemed the world.

*'If any man has a mind to come after me, let him
take up his cross daily and follow me.' Jesus goes
forward with great courage to do his Father's will:
'Thy will be done not mine.' He accepts the cross
to teach us how precious we are in the eyes of
God. His grace can transform every cross we meet
into a victory of love.*

LORD,

Your Gospel does not promise that we will be spared
from pain. Help us to understand that no matter
how we try to escape the cross it remains a human
reality, but your death and resurrection give meaning to it. You did not grumble about the heavy load.
Obediently you carried the cross without complaint.
Keep us from bitterness and despair. Teach us to
come prayerfully, in poverty of spirit, with open
hands. Give us the grace of acceptance and resignation. Help us to accept reality, to live with our
crosses and ourselves.

*Dying you destroyed our death.
Rising you restored our life.
Lord Jesus, come in glory.*

THIRD STATION
Jesus falls the first time

Then Jesus said , 'The hour has come for the Son of Man to be glorified. Truly I say to you, unless the grain of wheat falls to the earth and dies, it remains alone; but if it dies, it produces much fruit.'

John 12:23-24

We adore you, Lord Jesus Christ
and we bless you,
because by your holy cross
you have redeemed the world.

*Christ is now on his way to the hill of Calvary. The
road is long, the paved street is rough and the heat
of the noonday sun is overpowering. He arrives at
the foot of the hill. He has left the level ground and
starts to climb. It now becomes more difficult. He
grows weary beneath the heavy weight, stumbles
and falls.*

LORD,

Your first fall is like the fall of the young person on
the threshold of adolescence. There are many new
challenges and temptations now. Give courage and
strength to the young. Help them to avoid wrong-
doing. Protect them from drunkenness, drugs and
permissiveness. Teach them to handle their prob-
lems with gentleness, without panic or self-pity. The
Third Millennium will belong to them in a very
special way. Help those who lead them to build an
environment of love and trust where they can make
the right decisions for their future. When sin and
human weakness shatter their youthful idealism,
give them grace to rise from their fall and try again.

*Dying you destroyed our death.
Rising you restored our life.
Lord Jesus, come in glory.*

FOURTH STATION
Jesus meets his mother

Simeon blessed them and said to Mary, his mother, 'See him; he will be for the rise and fall of the multitudes of Israel. He shall stand as a sign of contradiction, while a sword will pierce your own soul.'

Luke 2:34-35

We adore you, Lord Jesus Christ
and we bless you,
because by your holy cross
you have redeemed the world.

*A mother meets a son. Mary encounters Jesus. It is
a soul-piercing experience. She is there at the right
time, in the right place. She offers encouragement
and sympathy, aware that her Son is fulfilling his
Father's will.*

MARY,

You were human, a woman who knew the pain
and hard knocks of life. Your son gave you to us to
be our mother. Gentle Mary, mothers are often torn
between anguish and hope, baffled at seeing their
children suffer, tempted to think that they have failed
their family and that God has abandoned them.
Give to women a calm vision of life. Teach them
their true role in modern society. May they be Christ-
bearers, evangelisers in the home, in the community, in the workplace, maintaining and restoring
life and love. Mary, gentle guide, Mother of the
Church, protect the gift of innocence in today's
youth. Take them by the hand and lead them back
to Jesus, your Son. Queen of peace, be with us
now and in the hour of our death.

*Dying you destroyed our death.
Rising you restored our life.
Lord Jesus, come in glory.*

FIFTH STATION
Simon
helps Jesus carry his cross

When they led Jesus away, they seized Simon of Cyrene, who was coming in from the fields, and laid the cross on him, to carry it behind Jesus.

Luke 23:26

We adore you, Lord Jesus Christ
and we bless you,
because by your holy cross
you have redeemed the world.

The cross is becoming heavy for Jesus. A passer-by is forced to help lighten the burden. Christ accepts gratefully. Christ needed Simon. That small gesture of charity would never be forgotten.

Lord,

We sometimes find it burdensome to involve ourselves with people. Teach us that the essence of Christianity is love; that every person is our neighbour. Let us see your presence in all people. Give us, O Lord, the grace and purpose to break through barriers of hatred; to plant seeds of love and forgiveness in barren places; to build bridges that will unite and sustain us spiritually in this New Millennium. Help us to recognise you especially in the poor, the sick and the elderly. May we do the menial tasks that no one else will take on. Make us humble enough to accept help from others. Thank you, Lord, for the good neighbours and friends who bring us sunshine, laughter and love.

Dying you destroyed our death.
Rising you restored our life.
Lord Jesus, come in glory.

SIXTH STATION
Veronica
wipes the face of Jesus

He was despised and rejected, a man of sorrows familiar with grief, a man from whom people hide their face, spurned and considered of no account. Yet ours were the sorrows he bore, ours were the sufferings he endured.

Isaiah 53:3-4

We adore you, Lord Jesus Christ
and we bless you,
because by your holy cross
you have redeemed the world.

A woman steps out from the crowd. Gently but courageously, Veronica wipes the face of Jesus. She braves threats, verbal abuse and even violence. In gratitude, Jesus signs her towel with the imprint of his face.

LORD,

Fear often makes us run away from demanding situations. Give us the strength not to be swayed by the company we are in, by the fashions of the times, by the desire to foolishly follow the crowd. Help us to speak out when Christian values are at stake. Give us the courage to follow our own consciences no matter what others may think or say. In this New Millennium keep us faithful to your teaching. Grant us the grace to accept the difficulties of sometimes having to stand alone in defending justice and truth.

Dying you destroyed our death.
Rising you restored our life.
Lord Jesus, come in glory.

SEVENTH STATION
Jesus falls the second time

How long, O Lord, will you forget me and hide your face from me? How long must I suffer pain in my soul and grief in my heart all the day long? How long shall my enemy triumph over me?

Psalm 13:2-3

We adore you, Lord Jesus Christ
and we bless you,
because by your holy cross
you have redeemed the world.

The second fall of Jesus might well be compared to the trials and stresses of middle-age. Christ is not as strong now as when he first began to climb the hill of Calvary. He stumbles and falls. But in rising again and struggling on, he challenges us to begin anew each time we fall.

LORD,

When we are drained and discouraged from continual frustrations and setbacks, give us the strength to accept ourselves with humble patience. A person is not a failure because she or he falls. When life seems to crumble and we imagine that we are useless and unimportant, help us to our feet again. Listen to the cry of our brokenness and confusion; help us to rise with dignity and begin anew. When we find forgiveness difficult help us to come back to the Church. May we return home and never again despair of your loving compassion. Let us pass this supreme hope on to others.

Dying you destroyed our death.
Rising you restored our life.
Lord Jesus, come in glory.

EIGHTH STATION
Jesus speaks
to the women and children

A large crowd of people followed him; among them were women beating their breasts and wailing for him, but Jesus turned to them and said, 'Women of Jerusalem, do not weep for me, weep rather for yourselves and your children.'

Luke 23:27-28

We adore you, Lord Jesus Christ
and we bless you,
because by your holy cross
you have redeemed the world.

*Along the Way of the Cross, there were women
who wept in pity. Jesus accepted their compassion
but mysteriously warned, 'Weep first for yourselves
and your children.' He foresaw the sad things to
come. People would choose to remain in sin and
reject the healing power of God's forgiveness.*

GOD OF MERCY AND COMPASSION,

Teach us that even if our hearts condemn us you
do not come to reject us, but to reveal yourself as
the God of immense tenderness and unparalleled
gentleness. In your providence, all things co-oper-
ate for good; even, in a mysterious way, our sins.
You gave us Jesus to be our Brother and Saviour.
May this new era mark a great return to the Father's House. May there be joy and celebration
when Christ welcomes back straying sinners. He
will embrace them in the Sacrament of his Mercy
and welcome them to the Table of the Eucharist.

*Dying you destroyed our death.
Rising you restored our life.
Lord Jesus, come in glory.*

How long shall the wicked, O Lord, how long shall the wicked exult? Pouring out words of arrogance, evildoers make a show of their insolence. They crush your people, O Lord, they oppress your inheritance. They murder the widow and the lonely, they massacre the helpless.

Psalm 94:3-6

We adore you, Lord Jesus Christ
and we bless you,
because by your holy cross
you have redeemed the world.

*It is difficult to be old in an uncaring world where
many feel that the aged have nothing to offer. This
station gives hope to the old, to the depressed and
to those who have given up on life. Christ is near
the end of the road and is completely drained of
strength. This time it is more difficult to rise. 'My
God, my God, why hast thou forsaken me?' But he
gets up and staggers on.*

LORD OF ALL HOPEFULNESS,

Bring to the sick your comfort and healing. Be to
the old and bedridden their stay and companion.
Teach patient tolerance to all that are no longer
young. Give to the dying the grace of perseverance
which you won for them in your third fall, the
assurance that when the final moments of life ebb
away you will come again and take them to yourself.

*Dying you destroyed our death.
Rising you restored our life.
Lord Jesus, come in glory.*

TENTH STATION
Jesus
is stripped of his garments

When the soldiers crucified Jesus, they took his clothes and divided them into four parts, one for each of them. But as the tunic was woven in one piece from top to bottom, they said, 'Let us not tear it, but cast lots to decide who will get it.' This fulfilled the words of Scripture: *They divided my clothing among them; they cast lots for my garment.*

John 19:23-24

We adore you, Lord Jesus Christ
and we bless you,
because by your holy cross
you have redeemed the world.

Jesus is stripped not just of his cloak but of his dignity, his respect, and his rights. Stripped and naked, our Saviour waits patiently for what is to come. He is a poor man and the poor must always wait. His nakedness challenges our affluent society with its false standards and shallow values.

LORD,

You know the loneliness of the empty chair, the parting with loved ones, the going away of children. Lord, help us when sickness seems to strip away our protections and nails us to a bed of pain. Strengthen us when all the support we have in life: family, health, possessions, – are taken away and we stand there raw and bleeding because these things have been so much a part of us. Lord, let us remember this moment of your passion and be consoled.

Dying you destroyed our death.
Rising you restored our life.
Lord Jesus, come in glory.

Jesus is crucified

People passing by shook their heads and insulted him, saying, 'Aha ! So you will destroy the Temple and build it up again in three days. Now save yourself and come down from the cross, if you are the Son of God.'

Matthew 27:39-40

We adore you, Lord Jesus Christ
and we bless you,
because by your holy cross
you have redeemed the world.

*Our eyes almost refuse to look on this most
appalling aspect of Christ's passion. Hammers are
raised, blows descend, and iron spikes tear their
way through his flesh. His muscles spasm and stiff-
en. The crowd taunt him with madness, failure and
folly. Jesus prays for his murderers: 'Father forgive
them...'*

LORD, OUR GOD,

We ask you to forgive us for the suffering that we
cause to others, for our lack of understanding, for
nursing grudges, for keeping up resentments, for
not admitting when we are wrong, for the bitterness and spite we often feel towards others. Create
a new heart in us, give us a spirit of reconciliation
and forgiveness. Where sin has brought division
and enmity, may your love bring healing and
strength; where sin has brought death, may the
grace of your passion and death bring new life.

*Dying you destroyed our death.
Rising you restored our life.
Lord Jesus, come in glory.*

TWELFTH STATION
Jesus dies on the cross

From midday darkness fell over the whole land until mid-afternoon. At about three o'clock, Jesus cried out in a loud voice, '*Eloi, Eloi, lamma Sabbach-thani*?' which means: My God, my God, why have you forsaken me?… Then Jesus cried out again in a loud voice and gave up his spirit.

Matthew 27:45-46,50

We adore you, Lord Jesus Christ
and we bless you,
because by your holy cross
you have redeemed the world.

Jesus, crying out in a loud voice, said, 'Father, into your hands I commend my spirit.' And having said this, he breathed his last. This is the Gospel passage that recalls the hour of supreme sacrifice. Love in all its beauty has reached a climax; the lover has given his life for his beloved.

LORD JESUS CHRIST,

Wounded healer and suffering servant, it is now my turn to bring help and healing to a broken world. You have no hands but mine; no face but mine that you can show to modern man. With Saint Francis, I pray that you will give me the grace to encourage rather than depress, to bring love where there is hatred, hope where there is despair, joy where there is sadness, light where there is darkness. Let the aim of my life be to comfort, to understand, to pardon and to love.

Dying you destroyed our death.
Rising you restored our life.
Lord Jesus, come in glory.

Jesus
is taken down from the cross

It was now evening and there arrived a wealthy man from Arimathea, named Joseph, who was also a disciple of Jesus. He went to Pilate and asked for the body of Jesus, and the governor ordered that the body be given to him.

Matthew 27:57-58

We adore you, Lord Jesus Christ
and we bless you,
because by your holy cross
you have redeemed the world.

Joseph and Nicodemus took down the body of Jesus from the cross and placed it in his mother's arms. Mary gazed at the wounds in his hands and feet and side. Christ still bears these wounds in his risen and glorified body. They are a pledge of his powerful intercession on our behalf before the throne of God.

LORD,

We look on your wounded hands. We think of our own hands, lazy, idle, sinful hands. Your wounded feet recall your journeys of mercy. We think of our feet that have often gone astray. Your wounded side reveals a heart that was broken for love of us. May your wounds help us to live with a sense of responsibility. Teach us to appreciate the Eucharist and Confession, to love you with intensity and sincerity. Grant us patience to accept our own wounds with resignation.

*Dying you destroyed our death.
Rising you restored our life.
Lord Jesus, come in glory.*

Jesus is laid in the tomb

So Joseph took the body of Jesus, wrapped it in a clean linen sheet and laid it in his own new tomb that had been cut out of the rock. Then he rolled a huge stone across the entrance of the tomb and left.

Matthew 27:59-60

We adore you, Lord Jesus Christ
and we bless you,
because by your holy cross
you have redeemed the world.

The hill of Calvary is a symbol of liberation and hope. Each new ridge we conquer opens up new insights into the beauty of God. The summit is it's prize: heaven, where the sun and scorching wind cannot touch us any more, where the Lamb will lead us to springs of living water, where God will wipe away all tears from our eyes.

LORD,

As we lay our loved ones to rest let us remember that pain and suffering have no power over them. Give resignation and peace to all that mourn. By your cross and resurrection you have set us free. Thank you for being a Saviour for each and every one of us. Yes, Lord, we firmly believe that you have gone to prepare a place for us so that where you are we also may be. We shall always be with the Lord. Let us console one another with these words.

Dying you destroyed our death.
Rising you restored our life.
Lord Jesus, come in glory.

Closing Prayer

LORD, GOD,

When our world lay in ruins
you raised it up again
through your passion and death.
Lord of the sun and the stars,
we celebrate with joy
the glory of your resurrection,
for through it
the world is flooded
with light.
All-highest, glorious God,
cast your light into the
darkness of our hearts.
Give us right faith,
firm hope and perfect charity
with wisdom and insight,
O Lord, so that
we may do
what is truly your will.

Jubilee Prayer

LORD,

May this time of Jubilee be a time of Hope for us. May it be a resounding hymn of joy and praise for the gift of Jesus, our Saviour, the Holy Spirit, our Sanctifier and the Father who wants to glorify us in eternal life. May it be for us a time of personal conversion and repentance, when we discover again, like the Prodigal Son, the amazing love and mercy in the Heart of our God.

May our celebration include a critical evaluation of our personal lifestyles, a recovery of the richness of your mercy in the Sacrament of Reconciliation and an opening of our hearts in compassion for the poor of the world.

In your firm embrace, O Lord, may we rest secure. In your gentle touch may our hearts be healed. Secure in you, may we reach out to bring your peace and joy to others. May all your children experience the gentle company of Mary most holy, Mother of the Church.

To you, O Father of life, eternal source of all that is, highest good and everlasting light, be honour and glory, praise and thanksgiving, with the Son and the Spirit for ages unending.

Amen